SIR CUMFERENCE
AND THE
VIKING'S MAP

COORDINATE
GEOMETRY

Cindy Neuschwander

ILLUSTRATED BY
Wayne Geehan

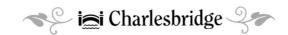

Charlesbridge

**To my grandson, Scott,
and my new granddaughter
on the way—C. N.**

**For my son, Jonathan, who is
mapping out his future—W. G.**

Text copyright © 2012 by Cindy Neuschwander
Illustrations copyright © 2012 by Wayne Geehan

At time of publication, all URLs printed in this book were accurate and active.
Charlesbridge, the author, and the illustrator are not responsible for the content or
accessibility of any website.

Published by Charlesbridge
9 Galen Street
Watertown, MA 02472
(617) 926-0329
www.charlesbridge.com

Library of Congress Cataloging-in-Publication Data
Neuschwander, Cindy.
Sir Cumference and the Viking's map / Cindy Neuschwander ; illustrated by Wayne Geehan.
    p. cm.
   ISBN 978-1-57091-791-2 (reinforced for library use)
   ISBN 978-1-57091-792-9 (paperback)
1. Coordinates—Juvenile literature. 2. Geometry, Analytic—Juvenile literature. I. Geehan, Wayne, ill. II. Title.
QA556.N478 2012
912.01'4—dc22   2011000865

Printed in China
(hc) 10 9 8 7 6 5 4 3 2 1
(pb) 10 9 8 7 6 5 4 3

Illustrations done in acrylic paint on canvas
Display type set in Realist by Graptail
Text type set in Adobe Garamond Pro by Adobe Systems
Color separations by Colourscan Print Co Pte Ltd, Singapore
Printed by 1010 Printing International Limited in Huizhou, Guangdong, China
Production supervision by Brian G. Walker
Designed by Martha MacLeod Sikkema

"We're well and truly lost," Per said to her cousin, Radius.
"How I wish we had a map." They were riding through a
forest in the late afternoon.

"Maps of Angleland are as rare as dogs with wings,"
replied Radius. "Maybe we'll be able to see where we are
at the top of that rise."

Together the two cousins rode up the hill.

"What a view!" exclaimed Per. The landscape below them lay divided into four sections. A road ran across the countryside horizontally, while a river wound through the area vertically.

"Hmm. Nothing looks familiar," observed Radius. "And we're running out of daylight. Let's camp on that knoll tonight. The grass there looks thick and soft."

As the cousins approached the knoll, a tangle of vines and brambles blocked their path.

"What's this?" asked Per, pulling aside some branches
to reveal a weathered wooden door. Together they pushed
it open and peeked inside. In the dim light they could
make out a musty room, full of cobwebs.

"It's a house inside a hill!" cried Radius.

Just then they heard the far-off sounds of raucous singing and laughter.

"Bad Old Barnaby and his brigand band:
We're the baddest lot in all the land!
We sneak and snatch whenever we can.
We're Bad Old Barnaby and his brigand band!"

In the distance they could just make out a ragged group of men marching along.

"Uh-oh!" Radius exclaimed. "Highway robbers!"

"Quick," said Per, grabbing a candle from her saddlebag. "Get inside the house."

Per shut the door and lit the candle. The room contained a bench, a barrel, and a round wooden shield.

While Radius examined the shield, Per peered into the barrel.

"What's this?" she wondered, pulling out an old, waxy leather pouch. She looked inside it. "A map!" The map was decorated with two unusual axes, each with two blades on either end of its handle. On the back was some writing. Per began to read.

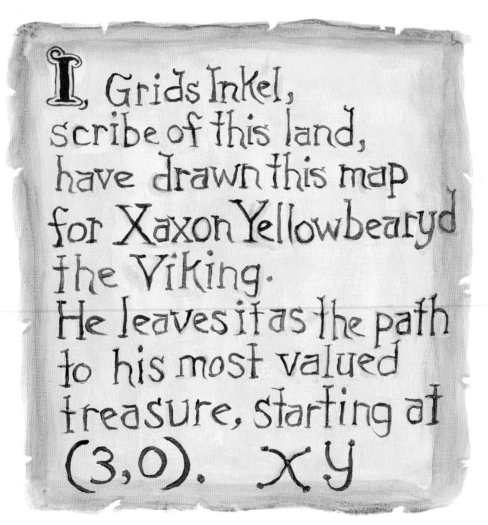

I, Grids Inkel, scribe of this land, have drawn this map for Xaxon Yellowbearyd the Viking. He leaves it as the path to his most valued treasure, starting at (3,0). x y

The ancient document was initialed by the Viking.
"Xaxon Yellowbearyd?" gasped Radius.
"Who was he?" asked Per.

"Only the fiercest Viking warrior ever! It was said he conquered most of Angleland," answered Radius. "I thought he was just a legend."

"I guess he was real," said Per. "Ready to look for his treasure tomorrow?"

"Absolutely," Radius said.

Early the next morning as they left the house in the hill,
Per noticed a flash of red between two nearby trees.

"What's that?" she wondered.

Radius shrugged. "A bird?"

Then they looked at the map and studied the land below.

"How do we read this?" wondered Radius.

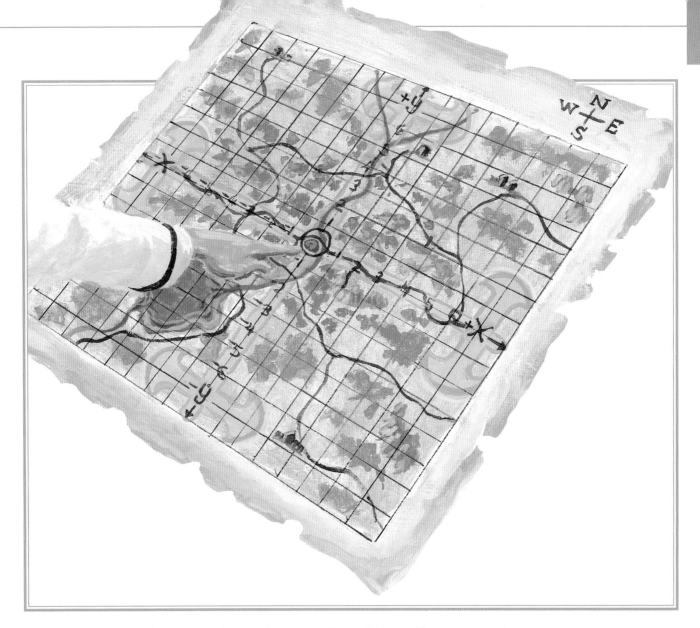

"Well, we're right here," said Per. She pointed to a picture of the house in the hill.

"But where do we go?" asked Radius.

"I think the numbers three and zero at the bottom of the message tell us," answered Per.

"There are two places on the map with three, but I don't see a zero anywhere," said Radius.

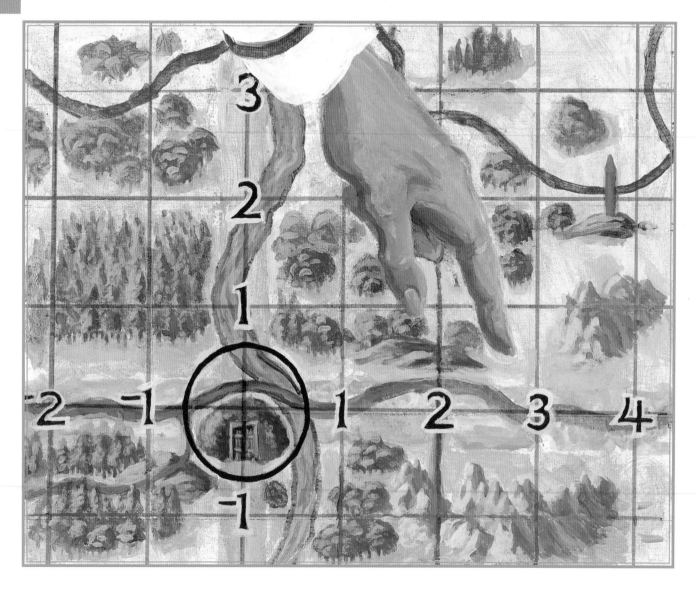

"The house in the hill looks like it's drawn inside a giant zero," said Per. "Let's ride up the river to the three there."

They trotted along next to the bank but didn't see anything unusual. After a while Per said, "This doesn't seem right. Let's go back where we started and follow the road out to the other number three." She traced her finger along the right horizontal X ax.

The cousins returned to the house in the hill and took the road, passing stone mile markers along the way. They stopped at the third one.

Per got off her horse and took a closer look. On the back of the marker, she noticed some small engravings.

"Radius!" she exclaimed. "I've found Xaxon's initials carved here, along with another set of numbers: (2, -1)!"

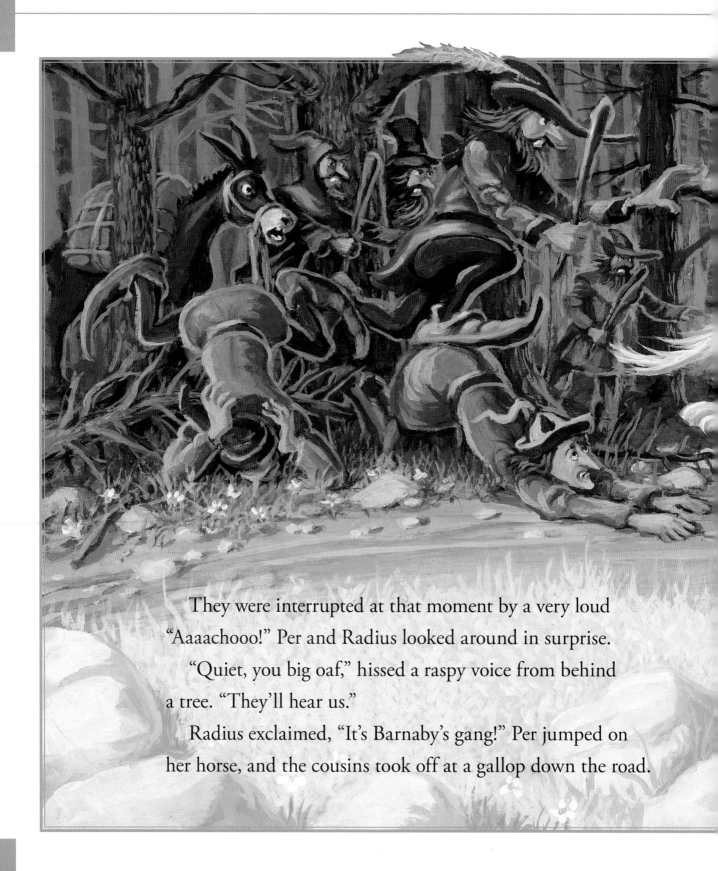

They were interrupted at that moment by a very loud
"Aaaachooo!" Per and Radius looked around in surprise.

"Quiet, you big oaf," hissed a raspy voice from behind
a tree. "They'll hear us."

Radius exclaimed, "It's Barnaby's gang!" Per jumped on
her horse, and the cousins took off at a gallop down the road.

After passing milestone six, they slowed to a walk.

"It isn't safe to go back," gasped Per.

"But we've got to," said Radius. "You were correct—the first number tells us which way to go on the X ax. If we want to get to the treasure we have to return to mile two on this road."

"If the first number tells us which way to go on the X ax," reasoned Radius, "the second number must tell us which way to go on the Y ax. It's like the alphabet—X comes before Y. The next set of numbers is (2, -1), so when we get to the mile two marker we'll go down the Y ax here." Using the guidelines he traced the way with his finger.

Together they galloped back down the dusty road, making
a hasty left turn at milestone two. They found themselves on
a narrow lane. Only then did they slow their horses to a walk.

"Did you see anyone?" Per asked Radius nervously.

"No," answered Radius. "I think we're alone."

The lane ended at the opening of a cave. "This must be our destination," said Radius, checking the map.

"We'll need some light in there," said Per, retrieving her candle. While the horses wandered off to graze, the cousins entered the cave.

"What are we looking for?" Per wondered. Candlelight flickered on the damp walls of the large cavern.

"I'm not sure," answered Radius, examining the far wall. Suddenly he paused. Carved into the wall were two more numbers: (-3,-3). "That's it!" he cheered.

But wait—did they hear voices and footsteps outside?

Per blew out the candle. "Crouch down," she whispered urgently.

The robbers entered the cave, all talking at once.

"Your sneeze chased them two young ones off."

". . . can't be far away."

". . . find the pelf. Maybe they have gold or coins."

". . . rest in this old cave first, and then . . ."

A stern, gravelly voice said, "Settle down, mates. Time
for a bit of shut-eye."

Soon loud snores could be heard.

Radius nudged Per. "Let's get out of here," he whispered.
They tiptoed toward the cave's entrance, past six snoring,
dark shapes on the cave floor. But just as they reached the
opening, Per tripped on a few loose rocks.

"Wha—what was that?" asked the gravelly voice.

Radius and Per dashed out of the cave and down the lane, the robbers stumbling after them. The two cousins whistled for their horses, then jumped onto their backs when they appeared out of the forest. They stopped only when they arrived back at the house in the hill.

"I think we lost them," said Per.

Radius nodded and pulled the map out of its pouch. Together they looked for (-3,-3). Radius ran his finger three markers along the left X ax, then three down the Y ax. "That's odd," he said. "It's in a lake."

After they had eaten and repacked their saddlebags, the two cousins continued their journey. They walked their horses carefully through the forest, and at last the lake came into view. They dismounted and walked to the water's edge to consult the map again.

"Aha!" said Radius, "(-3,-3) must be that large rock." He pointed a short distance into the misty lake. "Looks like we'll have to get wet."

But once again, Barnaby's band interrupted them. Six scruffy bandits burst through the trees and barreled toward them, waving sticks.

"They followed us again!" cried Per.

"Let's hope they can't swim!" Radius yelled, stuffing the map into the pouch. Together the cousins jumped into the water and paddled toward the rock.

"Follow 'em!" bellowed Barnaby. *Ka-sploosh!* The six men splashed awkwardly into the lake.

"Argh! Get off me, you big whale," one of the robbers gurgled. "I'm going under!"

While Barnaby's band floundered about, Per and Radius pulled themselves onto the big rock, gasping. As they did, a small boat appeared through the mist and glided toward them. A huge, gray Viking stood in its bow.

"A ghost!" screamed the robbers. They
stumbled out of the lake and fled to the forest.

"Xa—Xaxon Yel—Yellowbearyd?" stammered Radius.
"Looking for the treasure?" the ghostly warrior asked
in a gruff voice. Radius nodded, trembling. The Viking
motioned them aboard and took them back to the shore.

After Per and Radius disembarked, Xaxon gave each of them an ax just like the ones drawn on the map.

Then he handed them a small wooden chest. "This is treasure of the greatest measure," he growled. "Protect it." He pushed the boat away from the water's edge and disappeared into the mist.

The cousins stood on the shore, stunned. Then, slowly, they opened the chest.

"Maps of all of Angleland!" exclaimed Radius.

"This *is* a treasure," added Per. "We'll never be lost again." Then, thinking about Barnaby and his men, she shivered and said, "Let's get this to safety right away."

One of Xaxon's maps guided them back to the castle. Entering the courtyard, they came across Sir Cumference and Lady Di of Ameter, Radius's parents.

"Welcome back!" called out Sir Cumference.

"Yes," added Lady Di. "We were beginning to worry."

"We're fine. We found a cutting-edge map . . ." began Radius.

"And used some sharp thinking to get a handle on our location," finished Per.

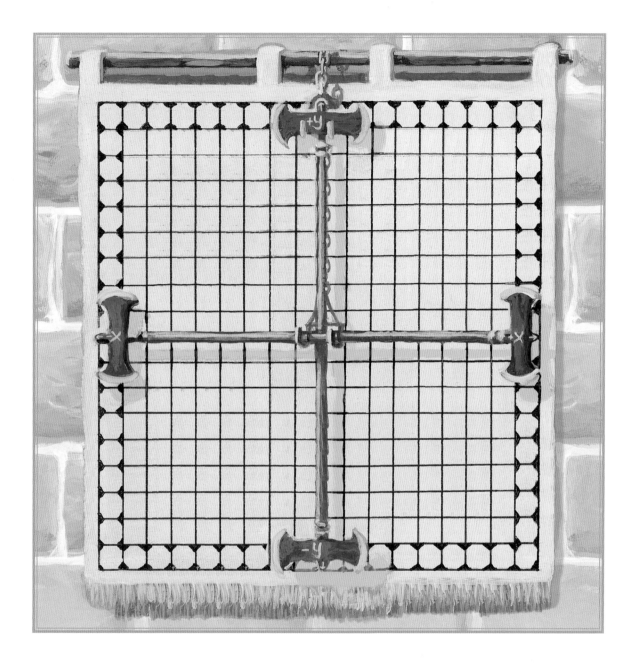

Epilogue

Xaxon's axes were hung in the Great Hall, and his maps were made into Angleland's first atlas. Eventually only the ax handles were drawn on maps. But everyone still referred to them as the "X and Y axes."

Mathematics that uses the X and Y axes is known as coordinate geometry or analytical geometry. It combines elements of geometry (the points on the grid) and algebra (the numbers used to locate the points). The numbers on the axes are both positive and negative. Where they meet in the middle, at zero, is known as the point of origin. A seventeenth-century French mathematician, René Descartes, developed the coordinate system we use today, although maps with coordinates had been used long before in ancient Greece.